Gemstone Guide Book

Gemstone Guide Book

A Simple Informative Handbook

J. Steele

Gemstone Guide Book
Copyright © 2015 by J. Steele. All rights reserved.

No part of this publication may be reproduced, stored in a retrieval system or transmitted in any way by any means, electronic, mechanical, photocopy, recording or otherwise without the prior permission of the author except as provided by USA copyright law.

Published By
Revival Waves of Glory Books & Publishing
PO Box 596
Litchfield, IL 62056

Revival Waves of Glory Books & Publishing is committed to excellence in the publishing industry.

Published in the United States of America

eBook: 978-1-312-79541-9
Paperback: 978-1-365-76350-2

Table of Contents

Introduction 7
ALEXANDRITE 8
AMBER 9
AMETHYST 10
AQUAMARINE 11
BLOODSTONE/ HELIOTROPE 12
APATITE 13
CITRINE 14
CORAL 15
CUBIC ZIRCONIA 16
DIAMOND 18
COLOURED DIAMONDS 20
EMERALD 21
FIRE OPAL 22
GARNET 23
IOLITE 24
IVORY 25
JADE 26
JASPER 27
JET 28
LAPIS LAZULI 29
LARIMAR 30
MARCASITE 31
MOISSANITE 32
MOONSTONE 33

MYSTIC TOPAZ	34
ONYX	35
OPAL	36
PEARL	37
PERIDOT	39
QUARTZ	40
RUBY	41
SAPPHIRE	43
COLOURED SAPPHIRES	44
SHELLS	45
NATURAL SPINEL	46
TANZANITE	47
TOPAZ	48
TOURMALINE	49
TIGERS EYE	50
TURQUIOSE	51
NATURAL ZIRCON	52

Introduction

Over the years J. Steele has worked with some of the best gems God's earth has to offer. He has now put this guide book together for all to use. This is a simple informative guide book. Buying colour gems is a challenge. Written for both consumers and professionals, it is easy to read, has colour photographs and gives practical pointers on how to decipher the differences. Whether you are interested in jade, opal, ruby, topaz, spinel, garnet, tourmaline or some other coloured gem, you will find this guide to be a fascinating and valuable resource.

ALEXANDRITE

Alexandrite is a variety of chrysoberyl that displays a colour change depending on light conditions and the angle it is view from (pleochroism). The ideal colour change would be fine emerald green to fine purplish red, but this is rare and expensive. Alexandrite was discovered in the Ural Mountains of Russia in the 1830's, and named after tsaravitch Alexander, the future tsar. That area was mined for over 60 years and still today Russian Alexandrite is considered the best quality. Today, small quantities of Alexandrite are mined in Brazil, Sri Lanka, India, Myanmar, Tanzania and Zimbabwe.

Colour: Green in daylight and red-violet in incandescent light.

Hardness: 8.5

AMBER

Amber is the fossilized resin from ancient forests. In ancient times the resin dripped and oozed down trees, filling fissures and trapping debris such as seeds, leaves, feathers and insects. The resin then became buried and fossilized through a natural polymerisation creating amber. The two main sources of amber in today's market are the Baltic states and the Dominican Republic. Amber from the Baltic states is older than that from the Dominican Republic is more likely to have insect inclusions. Most of the world's amber is in the range of 30-90 million years old. Semi-fossilized resin or sub-fossil amber is called copal.

Hardness: 2.5-3

AMETHYST

Amethyst is a transparent purple quartz. Origin of name from the Greek -amethystos- "not drunken". Amethyst was considered to be a strong antidote against drunkenness. Greek legend tells the story of a maiden Amethystos who was pursued a drunken god called Dionysus. She prayed to the goddess Artemis to remain chaste. The goddess granted her prayer, transforming her into a white stone. Filled with remorse Dionysus cried tears of wine over the stone turning it purple.

Different localities can produce a unique amethyst to that particular region or even to that particular mine. It is mined in Brazil, Uruguay, Bolivia and Argentina, Zambia, Namibia and other African countries. Very dark amethyst, mostly in small sizes, is also mined in Australia.

Colour: the colour range varies from pale lilac to deep purple.

Hardness: 7

AQUAMARINE

Aquamarine belongs to the gemstone family of Beryls. Origin of name Latin "aqua" meaning water and "mar" sea. Legend has it that Mermaids tails were made of aquamarine. Aquamarine is usually free of inclusions and possesses a superior brilliance. The more intense the colour of an Aquamarine, the higher its value. The principle supply of aquamarine stones comes from Brazil, Russia, Afghanistan, India and Pakistan

Colour: pale blue to light greenish

Hardness: 7.5-8

BLOODSTONE/ HELIOTROPE

Bloodstone or heliotrope, is a form of Chalcedony, a cryptocrystalline quartz. Bloodstone is green jasper with red inclusions. The red is sometimes caused by iron oxide or red jasper. Origin of name: From the red spots looking like spots of blood. It is usually cut "en cabochon" (that is shaped and polished usually with a flat bottom and a convex top) or into beads, it is used as a sealstone and in signet rings. Bloodstone is found in Australia, Brazil, China, India and the USA (Wyoming).

Colour: green with red inclusions

Hardness: 7

APATITE

Apatite is part of the phosphate mineral group. Origin of name: From Greek apate meaning deceit alluding to its similarity to other more valuable minerals such as olivine, peridot and beryl. Apatite is found in different worldwide locations like: Russia, Canada, Mexico, Spain and Africa.

Colour: varies from being transparent to opaque, with colours ranging from yellow, green, blue, violet and colourless.

Hardness: 5

N.B. This stone is very sensitive to heat and care needs to be taken.

CITRINE

Citrine is a form of quartz with ferric iron impurities and is rarely found naturally. Origin of name from the French word "citron" meaning lemon. Also called citrine quartz. Most commercial citrine is in fact heat treated amethyst or smoky quartz. Brazil is the leading producer of naturally mined citrine.

Colour: the different shades range from yellow, gold, orange brown shades of transparent quartz.

Hardness: 7

N.B. Citrine and Amethyst are the exact same minerals, the only difference is the level of oxidation of the iron contained in the mineral. As this can be done artificially by heat or irradiation a large majority of Citrine sold today is heat treated amethyst. There are currently no scientific ways to determine if Citrine was changed artificially.

CORAL

Precious coral or red coral is the common name given to Corallium rubrum. The hard skeleton of red coral branches is made up of mostly calcium carbonate and is durable and intensely coloured. Coral can be polished to a glassy shine. Usually deep water corals have light colour and shallow water corals have deep colour. Coral jewellery has been found in ancient Egyptian and prehistoric European burials and continues to be made to the present day. Due to its softness and opacity, coral is usually cut as a cabochon or used to make beads.

Hardness:3.5

CUBIC ZIRCONIA

Cubic zirconia or CZ is a synthetic variant of the mineral baddeleyite which is extremely rare in nature. It is the oxide of the metallic element zirconium, zirconium dioxide. It was first used in the Russian space program to serve as a window to photograph through, it was not used in jewellery until 1969 when somebody decided to facet the material. It is often used as a diamond simulant. Cubic zirconia should not be confused with zircon, which is a rare naturally occurring gemstone.

Colour: By adding other minerals in the creative process CZ's can come in any colour as well as the colourless variety.

Hardness: 8.25-8.75

N.B. Key features that distinguish CZ from diamond: Cubic zirconias have more dispersion than diamonds so show more fire. A CZ has a Mohs rating of 8.5-9 and Diamonds have a rating of 10. A CZ is 1.7 times heavier than a diamond of equivalent size. CZs are optically flawless whereas the majority of diamonds have inclusions or flaws CZ has a refractive index of 2.176, compared to a diamond's 2.417. CZ can be made in most cases entirely colourless: equivalent to a perfect "D" on diamond's colour grading scale but it is rare to find diamonds are truly colourless. CZs are thermal insulators whilst diamonds are among the most efficient thermal conductors.

DIAMOND

Diamonds are a form of carbon. Origin of name: From Greek for invincible.

What is a Diamond?

A diamond is a crystal completely made of the element **carbon**, except for trace impurities like boron and nitrogen. The arrangement of the carbon atoms or its **crystal structure** within the diamond gives it its unique properties. As well as being the hardest known material, it is also the least compressible, and the stiffest material, the best thermal conductor with an extremely low thermal expansion, chemically inert to most acids and alkalis, immensely strong, rigid structure with a very high melting point (3800°C) diamond is the hardest known natural substance.

Colour: it is rare to find diamonds are truly colourless.

Hardness: 10.00

COLOURED DIAMONDS

Diamonds come in all colours but these natural Fancy Colour Diamonds are rare and can be very expensive. One out of 10,000 normal diamonds is a fancy colour diamond. The colour of a fancy coloured diamond is measured differently to a normal diamonds. The grading scale is based on the intensity of the colour. The GIA fancy colour grading scale is: Faint, Very Light, Light, Fancy Light, Fancy, Fancy Intense, Fancy Vivid, Fancy Deep and Fancy Dark.

EMERALD

Emerald is a valuable Beryl that owes its colour to chromium or vanadium, which make it the bright green. Origin of name emerald is said to be a Sanskrit word meaning green (Sanskrit is a classical language of India). Emeralds can have many inclusions and flaws so can be brittle and liable to break. The value of an emerald depends on cut, colour, clarity and carat. Clear stones with vibrant colour command the highest prices. It is found in Brazil, Pakistan, Russia, East Africa, India, Madagascar and Columbia, at this point in time the best emeralds come from Colombia.

Colour: Emeralds come in many shades of green and bluish green.

Hardness: 7.5-8

N.B. Many emeralds are treated to hide surface-reaching breaks and improve transparency.

FIRE OPAL

Fire opal is a bright orange variety of opal.

It is primarily found in Mexico, so is often known as Mexican fire opal. Fire opal was known to the Aztecs between about 1200 to 1519 AD

Colour: Fire opals are transparent to translucent opals with warm body colors yellow, orange, orange-yellow or red.

Hardness: 5.5- 6.5

GARNET

Garnets are nesosilicates. 0rigin of name: from ancient Greeks as colour reminded them of the pomegranate seed or granatum. Garnets do not show cleavage (the tendency of crystalline materials to split along definite planes, creating smooth surfaces) so when they fracture under stress, sharp irregular pieces are formed. Because the chemical composition of garnet varies, the atomic bonds in some species are stronger than in others. The harder species are often used for abrasive purposes. It is found in the regions of Kenya, Sri Lanka, Thailand, Brazil, India, Madagascar, Canada, USA, Czech Republic and Spain.

Colour: virtually all colours

Hardness:6-7.5

IOLITE

Iolite is a blue silicate mineral that occurs as crystals or grains in igneous rocks, Origin of name: from the Greek ios, which means violet. Iolite changes colours (pleochism) depending upon which angle it is viewed from and the gems are cut to take advantage of that. It is found in Sri Lanka, Burma, Australia's Northern Territory, Namibia, Brazil, Tanzania, Madagascar, Connecticut, and the Yellowknife area of the Northwest Territories of Canada.

Colour: Transparent, violet-blue, light blue, blue, rich blue-violet stone

Hardness 7.5

IVORY

Ivory is a hard, white, opaque substance that is the bulk of the teeth and tusks of animals such as the elephant, hippopotamus, walrus, mammoth and narwhal. Ivory had been used for thousands of years for tools, implements and weapons and for carving and jewellery. The 1990 **Convention on International Trade in Endangered Species (CITES)** put a ban on international ivory sales to lessen the threat to endangered species by poaching. A species of hard nut sometimes called vegetable ivory or "tagua" is gaining popularity as a replacement for ivory.

JADE

The term "jade" refers to two different, yet similar semi-precious metamorphic mineral gemstones, Jadeite and Nephrite. Nephrite and jadeite are resistance to breakage and chipping and due to their toughness they made a superior weapons and tools for early man. Not until the 19th century that a French mineralogist determined that "jade" was in fact two different materials. Nephrite is usually only green and creamy white, while jadeite can have the full range of jades colours. Jade is mined in the regions of Canada, Australia, United States and Taiwan.

Hardness:6

JASPER

Jasper is microcrystalline quartz and is made from very small grains, it is a semi-translucent to opaque. Jasper has been used for thousands of years as tools and weapons during prehistoric times and for ornaments and jewellery later. Origin of name from the Greek iaspis. Jasper is commonly found in the regions of North Africa, Sicily, France, India, Venezuela and Germany, USA etc.

Colour: dark green, yellow, brown, green, yellow, red and white.

Hardness: 6.5 to 7.5

JET

Jet is a hard gem variety of Lignite. Jet is a type of brown coal, a fossilised wood of an ancient tree similar to our present monkey puzzle trees and cypress trees. These trees flourished in the Jurassic period when the trees died and fell they were eventually washed into rivers and seas to lie at the bottom for millions of years. All the other sediment built up causing great pressure, which flattened the wood and together with chemical changes altered the wood to jet. Jet has been used in Jewellery since ancient times and Queen Victoria wore Whitby jet as part of her mourning dress making it very popular.

LAPIS LAZULI

Lapis lazuli is an opaque to translucent precious gemstone composed mainly of lazurite and calcite. Origin of name from the Persian "lazhward", which was the name of a place in modern Turkestan known for its deposits of lapis lazuli ("stone of lazhward"). The finest colour is intense blue, lightly dusted with small flecks of golden pyrite. Polished Lapis can be made into jewellery. In the past it was also ground and processed to make the pigment Ultramarine for tempera paint and oil paint.

Colour: Deep azure blue to light blue, bluish green

Hardness: 5.5-6

LARIMAR

Larimar is a semi-precious blue variety of **pectolite**, Sodium Calcium Silicate Hydroxide. It was discovered in the Bahamas and Dominican Republic in the 1970's. The name "Larimar" comes from a combination of Larissa and Mar and was given to the stone by a Dominican who named the stone after his daughter Larissa and Mar, the Spanish word for sea. Although pectolite is found in many locations, none have the unique blue of larimar. This blue color, distinct from that of other pectolites, is the result of cobalt substitution for calcium.

Colour: pale blue to sky blue

Hardness: 5

MARCASITE

In jewellery, iron pyrite used as gem is improperly termed "marcasite" Origin of name from Arabic or Moorish for pyrite. Pyrite and Marcasite share the same exact chemical make up; however they both differ in their interior structure." Marcasite" is frequently found in inexpensive silver jewellery and watches. It was fashionable and popular in Victorian and other times where it was often used to imitate diamonds. In better quality jewellery it is hand-set with grains or beads of metal from the setting being pushed over the edges of the stones." Marcasite" occurs world-wide and is easily found in the chalk near Dover, Folkestone, and the French side of the English Channel.

Colour: metallic

Hardness: 6-6.5

MOISSANITE

Naturally occurring Moissanite was discovered in 1905 by Dr. F.H. Moissan, a French chemist and Nobel Prize winner and was named after him. Natural moissanite is very rare and is limited to iron-nickel meteorites. Virtually all of the moissanite sold in the world is synthetic. Synthetic moissanite is also known as silicon carbide after its chemistry (in industry moissanite is known as the man-made abrasive Carborundum). Moissanite is used as a diamond substitute as it is transparent and hard with a slightly higher refractive index than diamond. Moissanite jewels are cut to minimize their double refraction or birefringent effects. It is lighter and much more resistant to heat. This results in a stone of higher lustre, sharper facets and good resilience. Moissanite remains undamaged by temperatures used to melt gold.

Colour: rarely clear to shades of very pale green.

Hardness: 9.5

MOONSTONE

Moonstone is the best known gem variety of orthoclase feldspar. It is usually polished as a cabochon. Its importance as a gemstone arises because of adularescence, a floating light effect and sheen, compared to the light of the moon. This phenomena results from alternating layers of two kinds of feldspar, which cause light to scatter. Moonstone specimens commonly exhibit chatoyancy (a mobile, wavering striped reflection), and sometimes display a strong cat's eye.

Colour: most desirable colour of moonstone is blue, but it also occurs in grey, white, pink, green and brown.

Hardness: 6 to 6.5

MYSTIC TOPAZ

Mystic topaz is a treated clear topaz, it is not found naturally. To create mystic topaz, natural, colourless topaz is coated with a thin layer of titanium. The coating is only microns thick and is applied to the stones pavilion, the underside angled portion that typically forms the bulk of the gem. The specialized coating alters the stones natural refraction, creating rainbow colours, predominantly blues, greens, yellows, and small bursts of red shades.

N.B. this stone should be treated with care

ONYX

Onyx ia a chalcedony that occurs in bands of different colours. Onyx refers to a black and white banded variety of Agate and brown varieties are named Sardonyx. It is composed of relatively straight, parallel layers of different colours. This structure lends itself to cameo making.

It is usually cut into cabochon, or into beads, and is also used for intaglios and cameos. Some onyx is natural but much is produced by the staining of agate. It is available in the regions of USA, Germany, Brazil, Mexico, India, and Africa.

Hardness: 7

OPAL

Opal is a type of quartz. Origin of name: from Sanskrit (Sanskrit is a classical Indian language) upala = precious stone. They are luminous and iridescent with inclusions of many colours. Opals show a play-of-colour (a shifting of spectral colours)Opals are found in the regions of Mexico, Brazil, USA, Japan, Honduras, Kenya, Czechoslovakia, Peru, Canada but by far Australia is the main source of opals, almost ninety-five per cent of all fine opals come from the dry and remote outback deserts.

Colour: White, black, red, orange, most of the full spectrum, colourless, iridescent. Very infrequently of a singular colour.

Hardness: 5.5- 6.5

PEARL

Pearl is a smooth, lustrous, chiefly calcium carbonate organic gemstones. Natural pearls are nearly 100% nacre, a protective mother of pearl coating that is secreted to protect the organism for a foreign body that has entered the shell. Natural or real pearls come mainly from oysters, although there are other bi-valve molluscs which can produce them. Almost any species of bivalve or gastropod is capable of producing pearls. However, only a few species, such as the famous pearl oysters, can create pearls which are highly prized. Cultured pearls are produced by artificially introducing a foreign object into the fleshy part of oysters, which become coated with nacre in a similar manner to natural pearls. Imitation pearls, simulated pearls, have been produced for many years. Pearls are found in the regions of Japan, China, Tahiti, Australia, Indonesia, Philippines, USA and Burma.

Colour: white or cream, but the colour can vary according to the natural colour of the nacre in the various species of mollusc used. Can also be black or various pastel shades. Pearls (especially freshwater pearls) can be dyed yellow, green, blue, brown, pink, purple, or black

Hardness: 3.5 to 4.0

PERIDOT

Is the gem quality variety of the mineral olivine. Origin of name either the Arabic word faridat meaning "gem" or the French word peritot meaning "unclear". Peridot is one of the few gem stones that come in only one colour. The depth of green depends on how much iron is contained in the crystal structure. It is found in the USA, Myanmar, Egypt, China, Sri Lanka and Pakistan.

Colour: varies from yellow-green to olive to brownish green.

Hardness: 6.5 – 7

QUARTZ

Quartz is a crystalline rock or mineral composed of silicon dioxide. Quartz is the second most common mineral in the Earth's continental crust and found in all types of geological environment. There are 49 variety's, a number of which are gemstones, some of which are very beautiful and very rare. Origin of name from Saxon word Querkluftertz = cross-vein ore.

Colour: colourless, white, gray, yellow to brown to black, violet, pink

Hardness: 7

RUBY

Ruby is the red variety of the mineral called Corundum which is composed of aluminium oxide (any other colour of corundrum is a sapphire, see below). The red colour is caused mainly by chromium and titanium. It is natural for rubies to have imperfections in them, including colour impurities and inclusions of rutile needles known as "silk. Origin of name comes from ruber, Latin for red. Some rubies show a 3-point or 6-point star or asterism. These rubies are cut into cabochons to display this effect. Natural occurring rubies are very rare and extremely rare in large sizes over 3 carats. They can be found in many regions around the world from India, to East Africa, to South America, the Hindu Kush and a few deposits in the United States.

Colour: pinkish red or deep, rich red colour
Hardness: 9

N.B. Almost all rubies today are treated in some form (of which heat treatment is the most common practice) and rubies which are completely untreated and still of excellent quality command a large premium. Improvements used include colour alteration, improving transparency by dissolving rutile inclusions, healing of fractures (cracks) or even completely filling them.

SAPPHIRE

Sapphire is any colour of the mineral corundum other than red, those are called ruby, (see above) corundum is composed of aluminium oxide. Sapphires tend to be translucent or transparent and have high amounts of refraction. The most desirable sapphires are generally those with an intense blue colour with plenty of sparkle and life. Various shades of blue result from titanium and iron substitutions in the aluminium oxide crystal lattice. Some sapphires show a 3-point or 6-point star or asterism. These sapphires are cut into cabochons to display this effect. They can be found in Brazil, Tanzania, Sri Lanka, Kashmir, Thailand, Madagascar and Australia.

Colour: Shades of blue.

Hardness: 9

COLOURED SAPPHIRES

Sapphires are mainly known for their shades of blues, but they come in an assortment of colours.

Colour: all colours across the spectrum including white and black.

Hardness: 9

N.B. It should be noted that many Sapphires can be treated to enhance or change their colour. They are heated or irradiated to produce stronger colours such as greens, yellows or even blues. While the colour of Sapphires can be changed by intense heat and radiation, it is stable for daily wear jewellery.

SHELLS

Shells are organic minerals composed of calcium carbonate . Throughout the history shells of many types and from many different kinds of animals have been popular as human adornments. They are often used whole and drilled so that they can be threaded. The intricate design and varying colour patterns of shells is mainly dependent on the diet of the animal the shell covers. Mother of pearl or nacre is created by molluscs such as oysters and abalones secreting a substances that consist of calcium carbonate. Nacre is continually deposited onto the inner surface of the animal's shell creating the iridescent nacreous layer or mother of pearl. This is done both as a means to thicken, strengthen and smooth the inner surface of the shell. Mother of pearl has been used as decoration from buttons to inlays in furniture, jewellery and much more for thousands of years. Mother of Pearl can be found in many regions including Japan, Australia, Europe and the United States.

NATURAL SPINEL

Spinels are composed of magnesium aluminium oxide. Most Spinel is formed due to intense heat from volcanic activity or hydrothermal underwater streams. Origin of name: from Latin spinella meaning little thorn, after crystal shape. Spinels next to ruby and the rare red diamond, is the most expensive of all red gems. With a hardness of 8 and no cleavage planes, natural spinel is a tough and durable gemstone suitable for any kind of jewellery. Unfortunately most Spinel that is sold commercially is synthetic. Sri Lanka, Brazil, Thailand, and United States are most notable sources of natural spinel.

Colour: cobalt blue, red to blue to mauve. Dark green, brown, blackgreen, pink, deep pink with an orange tinge.

Hardness: 8

TANZANITE

Tanzanite is part of the zoisite mineral species and is only found in East Africa. Discovered in 1967 in the Umba Valley near the Usambara Mts. in Tanzania. Tanzanite may be colourless, yellow-green, brown, or blue to violet when found; the crystals are heat treated to enhance their colour.

Colour: Tanzanite is noted for its remarkably strong trichroism, appearing alternately sapphire blue, violet, and sage-green depending on crystal orientation. (Trichroism is the property possessed by certain minerals of exhibiting three different colours when viewed from three different directions under white lights. However, most tanzanite is subjected to artificial heat treatment to improve its colour and this significantly subdues its trichroism.

Hardness: 6.5

N.B: Tanzanite is a brittle stone and although it can be worn daily, care should be taken to protect it from knocks, pressure and extreme temperature changes. Do not use a home ultrasonic to clean jewellery with tanzanite

TOPAZ

Topaz is a fluorosilicate and can contain trace elements that cause different colours within the Topaz. Origin of name: from Greek Topazion, a Red Sea Island often covered in mist. Topaz wasn't really known about before the classical era, in the Middle Ages the name topaz was used to refer to any yellow gemstone. Deposits of topaz are found in the regions of Russia, Siberia, Brazil, Sri Lanka, Africa and China, Japan, Pakistan, Myanmar, Nigeria, Australia, Mexico, and in the United States.

Colour: Varies in a broad range of: yellow, blue, pink, peach, gold, green, red, and brown.

Hardness: 8

N.B. Topaz is often heated to change or enhance it's colour.

TOURMALINE

Tourmaline is one on the most complex gemstones of the silicate group and there are 10 different varieties created by the dozen or more elements they contain. Origin of name: from Sinhalese turamali = stone of mixed colours. There are Tourmalines, which change the colour from daylight to artificial light and others display chattoyance(a mobile, wavering striped reflection).Tourmaline is found in Africa, Brazil, Madagascar, Mexico, Myanmar, Namibia, Sri Lanka and USA.

Colour: depending on the variety green, red to pink, light to dark blue, colourless, purple , neon blue, brown, black, red to green and green to red.

Hardness:7-7.5

N.B. Tourmaline may be heated to enhance it's colour.

TIGERS EYE

Tigers Eye is mainly composed of silicon dioxide, it is a form of quartz that acquires fine golden lustre when polished. Origin of name: the stone resembles the eye of a tiger. Tiger's eye is a semi precious stone with a rich yellow and golden brown stripes that display chattoyance(a mobile, wavering striped reflection). Tigers eye is found in regions of South Africa and Western Australia.

TURQUIOSE

Turquoise is composed of aluminium phosphate and copper. Origin of name: from French for Turkish stone as in ancient days it was transported through Turkey. It was very popular during the days of Ancient Egypt and Ancient Persia and known to man since at least 6,000 BC. Delicate veining, caused by impurities, is desired by some collectors as proof of a natural stone. Turquoise is found in the regions of Iran, southwestern United States, Africa, Australia, Tibet, China, Siberia and Europe.

Colour: Blue, blue-green, green

Hardness: 5-6

NATURAL ZIRCON

Zircon is zirconium silicate, belonging to the group of nesosilicates. Origin of name: from Arabic zarqun and Persian zar = gold, gun = colour. Zircon is a natural forming mineral and it is not related to the synthetic diamond substitute Cubic Zirconium which is created in a laboratory. Zircon has a high refractive index and can be used to imitate diamonds. It is found in Australia, India, Brazil, and Florida, Cambodia, France, Myanmar, Thailand, Nigeria and Tanzania. Zircons found at Jack Hills in the Yilgarn Craton Western Australia are the oldest minerals found so far with an age of 4.404 billion years.

Colour: Zircon can come in red, brown, yellow, green, black or colourless. The colour of zircons below gem quality can be changed by heat treatment. Depending on the amount of heat applied, colourless, blue and golden-yellow zircons can be made.

Hardness: 7.5

www.ingramcontent.com/pod-product-compliance
Lightning Source LLC
Chambersburg PA
CBHW061108290125
21063CB00026B/361